REVIEW

"This book is amazing! The tools in this book have helped me to develop a better perspective on life. After reading this book, I am more self-aware of how I handle stress and able to manage it in healthy proactive ways. Truly life changing!"
- Ms. Maureen Amaral

"Manage Your Stress Master your Life by Certified Life Coach Lin Moctezuma is a book which is both timely and honest. The book provides useful information to all who seek a better way to handle life's stress. It's an enjoyable, easy read, that combines storytelling with practical advice for Stress Management. Proven and innovative techniques are combined with the goal of helping improve your life. This is a book that you will keep and refer to many times."
- Attorney Peter C. DiTomasso, Hartford, CT

"This book really helps if you want to start living a better, more stress-free life. It helps you analyze what you are giving the wrong attention to and what is making you feel overwhelmed, therefore, "blinding" your ability to dig deep and help take control of your feelings. I recommend this book

to anyone who needs an easy to read book with practical tips on how to deal with stress."
- Marisol Roberts

"Real solutions to real problems! This book hits home since it covers the things in life that we, as thinking, feeling beings, write off as taboo. Thank you for sharing."
- Michael & Marellys Hernandez

"It is amazing to see this book develop in many ways. It is powerful, very uplifting, and attractive to my mind, body, and soul."
- Gabriel Martinez

"*Manage Your Stress Master Your Life* is written in such a relatable way that it helped me do my own stress inventory and made me relook at some things in my life. This is a great reminder that stress offers both healthy and unhealthy aspects to my life. There are nuggets throughout this book that help identify patterns in your life and help you manage them."
- Krys Grant-Ray, Christian Transformational Life Coach, The Krys Grant-Ray Experience

"It is refreshing to see the way the author describes the issues many of us face on a daily basis and

give us ways of recognizing forms of stress and present strategies to cope with them. Using real life experiences from people like Amanda and her own experiences brings legitimacy to the author's work. This book brings you to look at yourself and question how you deal with certain situations. As you read it, you begin to see yourself in context to the issues presented and the strategies to cope with those issues. You will find yourself saying, "I have done that" or "I will definitely try that". I am sure the reader will enjoy it and appreciate what it has to offer to our daily lives."
- Mr. Luis A. Ramos, Sr

"The book is a great read on stress management based on a couple chapters. I cannot wait to read some more and use some of the tools in the book for the help of potentially managing my own stress."
- Diana Perez

"I absolutely love what I read! Great tips and advice for day to day and past life stressors and how to cope with them in the present. The writer is relatable because she shows results and cases from her professional life as well as her personal experiences. As a psychic medium, tarot reader, and tarot illustrator with so many projects at hand, it is amazingly

easy to get lost and disorganized. The type of work I do is not always welcomed with open arms and other's judgments can certainly affect me in some way, shape, or form. Lin points to meditation, which I do daily, as a tool to relieve stress, and this book adds an element of depth to help you deep within your core. Great self-help book with great tools."
- M.O. Vega, C.E.O. Arkana22

"WOW! I had the opportunity to read a couple of chapters in this book and I appreciate how the author provides details and various techniques on how to help you think differently. She helps you realize that it's ok to not be perfect and provides you with the tools that you need to learn how to handle any situation. Using the tools she provides, your life starts to change because your way of thinking gets healthier and so do you. I cannot wait for the release of this book as I am sure I will learn more tools I may want to practice. I want to thank the author for this as I am sure this will help a lot of people."
- William Perez, Owner of Xclusive Pest Control LLC.

MANAGE YOUR STRESS Master Your LIFE

Simple Tools and Daily Practices
to Free Your Mind, Go from Stress
to Calm, and Live Your Best Life

Lin Moctezuma

Powerful You!
PUBLISHING
Sharing Wisdom ~ Shining Light

Manage Your Stress Master Your Life

Simple Tools and Daily Practices to Free Your Mind, Go from Stress to Calm, and Live Your Best Life

Copyright © 2020

Published by: Powerful You! Inc. USA
powerfulyoupublishing.com

Library of Congress Control Number: 2020913103

Lin Moctezuma – First Edition

ISBN: 978-1-7328128-9-5

First Edition August 2020

SELF-HELP /Self-Management/Stress Management

Dedication

Luis, Nuni, and Jazlin, who have been supportive and patient with me through this writing process and continuously remind me how much I am loved and appreciated.

Table of Contents

Introduction

Stress and feeling stressed out are highly con-
tagious, so by taking time to recharge regularly
we can have calm energy that helps others
around us calm down too.

Is it possible to let go of things we have no control over and focus on the positive things in
life? In other words, is there really such a thing
as "stress management?" As I have learned, both
through personal experience and my work as a life
coach, the answer is yes. Stress is inevitable, but
we can most certainly mitigate its effect on our
wellbeing. We can even learn to use stress to learn
more about ourselves and improve our health, relationships, and careers. This is where I come in.

The ability to remain relaxed and focused in
tense situations is a vital aspect of stress management. If you don't know how to stay centered and
in control of yourself, you may become emotionally
overwhelmed. While it will ultimately be up to you
to gather the strength to make the changes, in this

book I will give you tools to help you manage stress in your life and the feeling of overwhelm that often accompanies it.

What is Stress?

Stress is a situation where the demands on a person exceed his/her ability to cope. It triggers strong emotions and can lead to hurt feelings, disappointment, discomfort, overwhelm, and frustration. When handled in an unhealthy manner, it can cause a host of physical and mental symptoms and may even irreparably damage our relationships.

While there is literally an endless number of things that can stress us out, stress is essentially caused by two things: your belief that a given situation warrants anxiety; and the way your mind and body react to such thoughts.

Have you ever wondered why you always seem to get sick right around the holidays or cannot sleep on Sunday nights when you have to get up early for work the next morning? Stress may very well be the answer. Stress has many negative effects on the physical body and, many studies show, can even lead to serious illness. Some of the well-known effects of stress include:

- Headache
- Stomachache

- Rapid breathing
- Depression
- Immune system response
- Heart disease
- Insomnia
- Tension and body aches
- Infertility
- Irregular menstrual cycle
- Gastric ulcers and other digestive problems

Stress also affects us emotionally and mentally. Prolonged stress can lead to depression, causing us to lose focus on ourselves and what really matters. We are quick to react to otherwise benign situations and may lash out at our spouse, kids, or other family members, as well as co-workers and friends. Stress wreaks havoc with our eating habits, causing us to overeat, lose our appetite, and make poor food choices. We may also turn to smoking, alcohol, or medications as a way to cope with what we are going through. Of course, none of these are effective and oftentimes lead to more problems for us to deal with. The good news is that there are a number of simple but effective tools that will help you get the better of stress before stress gets the better of you.

The following chapters contain examples from my personal life and my coaching practice about the causes and effects of stress, as well as several tools I have found effective in managing that stress. It is my sincere hope that the anecdotes will help you identify your stressors and see them from a new perspective, and that the tools will assist you in both calming and invigorating the body, mind, and spirit.

Chapter 1
Managing Stress through Journaling

Journaling is a great practice for overall stress reduction, as well as self-knowledge and emotional healing. Writing down your thoughts, feelings, goals, fears, dreams and so on creates a deeper connection between your everyday conscious self and your true inner self. It helps you process and deal with negativity by literally getting it out of your system and onto the page.

We have all heard the saying, "No use crying over spilt milk," meaning it is fruitless to get upset over something that has already happened and is therefore out of our control. Its earliest known use was back in 1659, in a book called *Paramoigraphy: A Book of Proverbs in English, Italian, French and Spanish,* yet three-and-a-half centuries later we still struggle to remain calm in the face of stressful situations.

I came across a more literal example of this in

one of my stress management workshops, when a tearful young woman (we'll call her "Debbie") raised her hand and asked, "How do I not stress when my daughter spills the last little bit of milk we had left, and I can't afford to provide food for my kids?" Her question certainly got the room's attention! Not only was it heart-wrenching, it also drove home the point that we never know what someone else is going through and should not judge their "spilt milk."

After sharing that she was also going through a divorce, Debbie went on to say that when her daughter spilled the milk, she wanted to yell at her but knew it was not the best way to handle the situation. What, she wanted to know, could she do to manage her stress in a way that was healthy for her and her children?

"Well, you are in the right place," I replied, "because in this workshop I will give you tools to do that."

Yet as I continued with the class, I couldn't help but notice the look of sadness on Debbie's face. She listened intently to everything I said about stress management, all the while scribbling notes. Clearly there was something deeper going on than she had revealed to the class.

Not wanting to put her on the spot in front of

everyone, I told her I would l be more than happy to speak with her privately after the class. I wasn't the only one who noticed her despair, for as soon as the workshop ended Debbie was surrounded by people talking to her and hugging her. She looked so overwhelmed and, not wanting to pressure her further, I decided to wait for her to come to me. I went around the room, thanking everyone for coming and giving them my business cards. It wasn't until I began cleaning up the room that Debbie came over and thanked me for the helpful class.

Seeing an opening, I in turn thanked her for having the courage to share what was obviously a very painful topic. I then reminded her to shift her focus from the things she couldn't control—the "spilt milk"—to what was working in her life. This is the way we begin to learn to better manage our stress. Debbie seemed receptive to my advice, and indeed we soon began private sessions to start her on the road to effective stress management.

Everyone experiences challenges differently. When we have resources to call upon, we feel confident; when we lack resources, or believe we lack them, it seems that things are spiraling out of control. This leads to stress and feeling overwhelmed. To change this dynamic, we need to find our own unique strengths. As we go through this process, we often realize that our stress level, and our ability to manage it, has a direct correlation to our perception of the problems we face.

The first step is to gain insight into the underlying emotions and beliefs that are contributing to our stress and perhaps informing the way we handle it. Your mental, emotional, and physical state filters how you look at life. Many of us know this, yet sometimes it is difficult to discern whether our emotions are causing a situation or if it is the other way around. In my coaching practice, I encourage all my clients to journal, as this is an excellent way to understand our emotions and release those that are not serving us. I usually find it helpful to ask my clients a series of questions about their journaling, for example:

- What do you write about in your journal?
- When do you write?
- How do you feel after you journal?
- Do you feel like you can journal your feelings and leave them on a piece of paper, or do you continue to carry that weight around?

You can also ask yourself these questions. When you do, dig deep inside for the answer, and remember to always be honest with yourself, for that is the only way this process will work.

In my sessions with Debbie, I noticed that she was journaling about all the good things that had happened throughout the day, but never about the negative. When I asked her why she did that, she replied that she did not want to go back and relive those experiences. I could certainly understand that. It seems contradictory to tell people to focus on the good in their lives and then tell them to journal about the bad. However, there is a big difference between dwelling on the negative and stepping back and examining it from a broader perspective.

When you are feeling stressed out, it can be extremely helpful to look at the big picture, almost as if you are looking at your life from the outside. Ask yourself questions like, *What does this situation really mean? How much of this do I have control over and what can I let go of?*

Sometimes you may find that you are stressed out over things you fear will happen. As the Roman philosopher Seneca said, **"A man who suffers before it's necessary, suffers more than is necessary."**

As we discussed her journaling, Debbie realized that she was letting go of the good feelings by writing them down and holding on to the negative feelings by harboring them inside. When you write all your stresses, negative feelings, and emotions down, do not go back and read it. Simply turn the page to a new one. We must do that in life as well; we have to be able to turn the page of whatever situation we are going through in order to move forward.

Any time something good happens, put your hand over your chest and just sit with that feeling. As you let the feelings of joy flow through your body, focus on your gratitude and appreciation for it. Set your intention to carry these feelings with you throughout the day.

On the other hand, when you're stressed about any situation, having a bad day, or feeling negative, angry, frustrated, or hurt, it's time to pull out the journal.

Before sitting down to write, take a moment to ask yourself the following questions, and remember, no one will see this but you so be completely honest with your answers.

- What are you trying to prove (with regard to the particular situation)?
- What are your beliefs about life, as they pertain to what is currently stressing you?
- What feelings or emotions come up for you when you think about a particular person?
- What beliefs do you have that are limiting your happiness or getting in the way of what you truly want?

These questions will help you uncover the real emotions behind your stress and understand them in a different way. I find it is helpful to combine journaling with a regular meditation practice, such as the one described below.

Meditation:

Sit quietly in a place where you will not be disturbed. Be sure to turn off your phone, computer, television, et cetera. Begin by focusing on your breath, deeply inhaling and exhaling. If a person or event in the day has upset you, reflect constructively on those situations. Examine what emotions are coming up, close your eyes and notice what sensations you have in your body.

Focus your attention on the part of your body that feels the feeling; describe the feeling. For example, is it a pit in your stomach? Tightness in your chest? Grinding of your teeth? Is it an overall feeling, like fatigue? Are you upset? Angry? Frustrated? Disappointed? What part of your body is feeling these emotions? Send love to that part of the body and thank it for helping to make you aware of your feelings.

Now, return to your thoughts. When we are feeling stressed, we tend to overthink the situation, and the thoughts usually involve limiting beliefs.

Meditation is a great way to replace the negative thoughts or self-talk with positive statements. You might try choosing one as a mantra and repeating it over and over, for example, "I know how to deal with this; I've done it before."

Chapter 2
Triggers - Identifying and Neutralizing Them

As the name suggests, a trigger is something that sets off a reaction of stress, pain, or anger. A trigger can be anything from a word or event to a particular person or even a song playing on the radio. Our triggers are our wounds—the more hurt we've endured and the weaker our boundaries, the more reactive we are. When we react negatively, we allow ourselves to be taken over by someone or something outside of us, which usually results in the escalation of hurt feelings, conflict, and our stress level. Oftentimes, however, we're not really reacting to the present person or situation but to something or someone from our past. We are a product of our environment, including pain and frustrating things we experienced while growing up. Some of these things stick with us and, if not dealt with, can continue to trigger emotions well into adulthood. These emotions—positive, negative, or neutral—are determined by the meanings or interpretations we attach to events in our lives. When we are triggered, it is not because of the experience itself, but our interpretation of that experience.

Here are just a few examples of emotional triggers:

- Someone criticizing you
- Someone being unavailable to you
- Someone leaving you or threatening to leave
- Someone trying to control you

Getting "triggered" is an opportunity to heal and grow. Once we understand this, we can begin to recognize and disarm the triggers so they no longer have power over us. We can also start to look at our lives from a new, healthier perspective, which prevents new triggers from forming.

In the words of Rupi Kaur, "How you love yourself is how you teach others to love you."

We are typically so busy moving through our daily activities that we don't take the time to check in with ourselves. We have also become very adept at ignoring the clues our bodies are giving us throughout the day. For example, it's past five o'clock and you still have a pile of work to do. You're debating staying late at the office when you notice tension in your neck and shoulders. This can be your body's way of telling you, "Hey, this is stressful, let's take a break!" You might get up and stretch or get a glass of water, or you might decide to leave, get some rest, and start fresh in the morning. Identifying triggers can be a big step toward becoming more connected with yourself and learning how to neutralize them. It's important to check in with yourself from time to time, to see what your body is trying to tell you or what it is you need at that moment.

When we are going through stressful situations in our lives, it's easy to focus on what is not going well. When we do this, we are actually triggering our own emotions. Give yourself a break! Yes, there will be opportunities to grow and change, but be sure to create some space to acknowledge what is working. You have talents, gifts, and skills; don't be afraid to acknowledge and use them! Remember, you don't have to be perfect to be awesome.

The first step in healing triggers is being able to identify them, as well as your internal beliefs. You do this by paying attention to your feelings. When you notice that you are being triggered, try to take a mental step back and see what that trigger might be. Then you begin to learn how to take the charge out of that trigger. You must also be able to name what you feel and need in order to communicate effectively. Sharing our feelings when we are triggered takes courage, however, keeping our feelings inside only makes things worse. That said, you should be mindful of who you express your feelings to. Not everyone can help you handle these feelings appropriately, so you may want to ask someone outside of the situation.

There was a time when I did not know what a trigger was, let alone what triggered me and why. It took time and some work before I was able to identify my triggers, and even more time and effort to neutralize them. This is not a quick fix, but it is one of the most worthwhile things you will ever do for yourself.

Remember that these are wounds, so approach them with compassion and tenderness. Depending upon what the trigger is, healing may involve the stages of grief and/or re-evaluating the context and validity of learned beliefs.

> *"Instead of resisting any emotion, the best way to dispel it is to enter it fully, embrace it and see through your resistance."*
> ~ *Deepak Chopra*

Don't be so hard on yourself. If you have been triggered by someone or something, give yourself permission to feel that feeling. Intense feelings often last for ninety seconds, so if you can hang on and "ride the wave" for that short period you'll start to notice a more peaceful feeling. Then, once you are out of the heat of emotion, you can begin to look at the situation from a new perspective.

Healing our triggers means learning not to obsess about things beyond our control, as this leads to feelings of powerlessness (another trigger). For example, we can't control other people's reactions, especially when we are expressing what is triggering us. I am not suggesting you pretend to be happy when you feel stressed, anxious, or upset, but that you understand that you can nurture and sustain yourself, no matter how they react. It's important to deal with negative feelings, but also try to focus on the positive things in your life too.

Self-awareness is one of the steps of personal transformation. Only when you understand yourself and the unconscious obstacles, including triggers, that you've been wrestling with, can you make the changes that will help you break free.

Here are some ways to become aware of and neutralize your triggers:

- Calm your mind and body through meditation, listening to music, exercising, or anything else that makes you shift your focus away from the triggering event.

- Develop regular self-care routines such as eating healthy, getting enough sleep, and exercising to get rid of pent-up tension.
- Listen to your body's cues; for example, when you notice tension in your shoulders, roll them back and forth and say to yourself, "I am resilient and can make it through this stressful day."

Chapter 3
Overwhelming Stress
Change Your Words,
Change Your Life

A client of mine (we'll call him Bob) reached out to me one day and said, "I am over-whelmed with stress. I need help prior-itizing, organizing, and getting things done in a way that doesn't feel so overwhelming." When I asked him what he was overwhelmed with, he re-plied, "Just with everything." I then asked Bob if he could pinpoint one thing, and he said, "Stress. I am stressed about everything and I don't know how to move forward with the things I must do because it's a long list."

I realized that Bob was generalizing and attribut-ing his feelings to stress without really delving into them or the real reason for his feeling overwhelmed. He's not alone. Many of us use quick and easy labels to describe our feelings. Stress management is not just about how to handle stress but about learning to differentiate our emotions and use the right words to describe them. Why? Because the words we attach to our experience actually *become* our experience.

I quickly learned that Bob was a person who stressed very easily, and over our many sessions I had to take a gentle approach so as to not overwhelm him.

I asked him to make a list of all the things he wanted to get done. It included managing money better so he'd be able to take his family on vacation and work on a series of house projects that he had been putting off. I then asked him to look at his list and tell me what the most important thing was. He said it was taking his family on vacation. When I asked him what he was struggling with the most, the answer was managing his money. He wasn't sure what he was doing wrong, but he had not been able to save; this was making him feel overwhelmed, because he had so much to do in his house and didn't have the means to do it all. To Bob's surprise, I told him that he had made progress. By simply writing these things down and acknowledging what he wanted and what his struggle was, he was able to take a small step toward overcoming what he referred to as overwhelming stress. I am happy to say that Bob is managing his stress much better and using the tools to work through the feelings of overwhelm when they do arise.

*"Life has a way of testing a person's will,
either by having nothing happen at all or by
having everything happen at once."*
~ Paulo Coelho

Overwhelming stress is real. We often get so caught up in our to-do list and other obligations that we lose sight of the purpose of accomplishing any given task. When I work with my clients who are experiencing "overwhelm," I go slow with them. I move at a pace that makes them feel comfortable yet accomplished, even if it's by taking one very small step at a time.

My next step was to have Bob define his personal purpose and values. Your purpose is what you want to accomplish, for whom, and to what end. Whether we realize it or not, we all have a purpose. Purpose is "present-oriented" while your vision is "future-oriented," so your focus should be on the work you are putting in and the opportunity that today offers. Values, defined in behavioral terms, enable you to be clear about how you'll go about accomplishing your goals.

Sometimes you need to relax, breathe, let go, and just live in the moment.

The quality of your life is determined by where

you live emotionally and, as mentioned earlier, the words we use have a tremendous impact on how we feel. By simply changing the words you consistently use to describe emotions, you can change how you think, feel, and live. This is called "transformational vocabulary." When I made a conscious decision to practice it each day there were people who talked about me, judged me, and even made fun of me. That's okay, though, because I've observed its power firsthand. Changing just one key word when communicating with others can instantly change the way they feel—and how they behave.

Remember, we intensify our experience of stressful situations through the way we look at them. If you can look at your situation differently, you may be able to put it into a different perspective—one that causes you less stress! Of course, to do this takes work, dedication to the process, and the strong desire to change; it requires you to look your *fear* of change in the eyes and tackle it head-on.

If you want to transform your life, if you want to shape your decisions and your actions, shifting your emotional patterns are the key. Again, a tool that can change it faster than anything else is consciously selecting the words you use to describe how you feel or when communicating your feelings.

Be prepared for life's troubles but remember that

things don't happen to you—they happen *for* you. Release the mistakes of the past and carry forward only the lessons they contain. You are not your past or your mistakes. You always have a choice.

Surround yourself with those who honor the best in you and with those who lift you up. Your mental health is comprised of your social, psychological, and emotional states. There are a lot of ways you can improve your mental health on your own, including monitoring your mood, engaging in self-care, changing your physical activity, and participating in social activities. The best thing you can do for your mental well-being is recognize that your current state is not permanent.

See every interaction as a path to growth. Look at every life experience as an opportunity to do better and be better. Discover your unique passion and purpose and bring it forward to make a difference in the world. Believe in the power of forgiveness. Embrace change.

Most importantly, love yourself and be grateful for the life you have. This is how you create a level of choice, rather than a reaction that you follow on autopilot.

Transformational vocabulary gives you the power to change your experiences in life by taking the most negative feelings you experience and lowering their intensity to the point where they no longer control you. It also can be used to take positive experiences and elevate them to even greater levels of pleasure.

Choosing different words announces your intention to start living a more positive, happy life; it also helps you create other beneficial habits that will bring about positive changes.

When we label our emotions accurately, we are able to determine the precise course of our feelings. Every single emotion that we feel has a meaning behind it. We can't always stuff our emotions away just because they are negative emotions, and we can't put a label of "stress" on every negative emotion we feel or situation we go through. When we realize that our emotions, even the difficult ones, are trying to tell us something, and when we cultivate the ability to sit with them and trust the process, our emotions lose their control over us.

Everyone gets overwhelmed from time to time, but it doesn't need to lead to anxiety or excessive stress. The key is to make sure that you stay in the moment, pick your priorities, accept imperfection, and recognize that everything is an opportunity for growth.

Big tasks, projects, and plans can seem daunting. They may even invoke feelings of dread, oftentimes because they seem unmanageable. The next time you have such a task, take some time to write down what you need to do to complete it. Break it down into much smaller subtasks that you can do easily. You don't need to plan your entire journey in one sitting. When you are only focused on the next step, your stress surrounding the entire task will dissipate.

This leads us to an important caveat: resist the urge to multitask. Multitasking can seem like the best solution, but in reality, it divides your focus and prevents you from being efficient. You lose valuable time in the process of shifting gears, rather than spending it on your actual purpose. If you do have multiple things to do, don't worry. Just give yourself a timeframe to work on each task before moving on to the next. If things pile up and you start to feel overwhelmed, don't panic. Remember to stop and be mindful of the present moment, as this gives you a break from the thoughts and concerns that cause anxiety. Quieting your mind and moving away from the endless "what-if" scenarios helps to center you in the present and prepares you to deal with the tasks that lie ahead more effectively. No matter how talented or motivated you are, it's impossible to do everything at once. The best way to dig yourself out of an overwhelming situation is to pick your top priorities and work from there.

Prioritization is difficult for many because at first

glance everything seems equally important. When we step back and practice mindfulness, however, we realize that isn't the case. It's always possible to prioritize things in your life. Confront and accept the reality of imperfection. It's far better to recognize that we live in an imperfect world and that sometimes our best effort is good enough, even if it too is imperfect. This applies to both work and personal life.

Sometimes it's better to let the housework slide so you can play with your children or to relinquish control on a project rather than micromanage it. Learning to accept imperfection enables you to keep moving forward, and that is precisely what you need to do when you are feeling overwhelmed.

We must also learn to recognize and escape what I call "thinking traps"—this is when our mind convinces us of something that is not true. Black and white thinking falls into this category: we view something as either good or bad, a success or a failure. For example, "I planned on going to the gym and eating a healthy meal today, but I didn't so my goal of losing weight is ruined."

The reality is you have not failed, you had a small setback. All you must do is get back on it the next day.

Another common trap is when we take our emotions as evidence of truth; for example we think of something as negative so it makes us feel bad, or we think we are responsible for the pain and happiness of everyone around us. The way to change this is to improve our mindset and change our words from negative to positive affirmations.

Try this ten-day challenge: First, identify the emotions, the feelings, and the stress that you experience most often. Then, find a new word or words that help you to break your pattern of thought and feeling. Avoid "I am" statements because these are powerful identifiers and will further bind you to the emotion. Instead use words like "I am noticing that…"

Chapter 4
Stress: It's Not Just for Adults

They may not be dealing with all we've got on our plates, but children can and do get stressed. School, friends, and family dynamics are just a few things that can lead to feelings of anxiety and overwhelm. As kids do not know how to articulate what they are feeling, their stress may present in other ways, such as changes in sleep patterns, behavior, and eating habits, whether it be overeating or not having much of an appetite. Moreover, as children model their parents' behavior, how they deal with that stress largely depends on what they observe in the home. Parents who deal with stress in unhealthy ways risk passing those behaviors to their children. Alternatively, parents who cope with stress in healthy ways not only improve their own quality of life, they also promote the formation of critically important habits and skills in their kids. Yes, changing our behavior is challenging, but look at it this way: what better reason could there be for doing so than to become positive role models for our children?

> *"Families are like fudge—mostly sweet, with a few nuts."*
> ~ Les Dawson

Stress management is indeed a family affair and talking to your children to promote open communication and problem-solving is an important part of that. Low levels of parental communication have been associated with poor decision-making among children and teens. Having regular conversations can help a family work together to better understand and address any stressors children are experiencing.

There are many other changes you can make to reduce stress in your household. How you go about doing this is up to you; for example, you might want to make several important changes at once (i.e. eating healthier foods, being more physically active, getting a better night sleep, or spending more time together). If you are already overextended from juggling many different responsibilities, you might instead choose to start with one behavior. Your family will be more likely to experience success, which will encourage you to tackle other challenges. Whatever route you take, it might be helpful to break it down into manageable steps, and to keep in mind that changing behaviors takes time and patience.

I know firsthand just how much we pass on to our kids. One day, my son called me in tears; he had to leave work because he was experiencing severe anxiety and having trouble breathing. By the time he got home the anxiety was so bad that he was hyperventilating. I had to do something quickly, and though my first instinct was to mother him I knew that at the moment this was not what he needed. I had to dig deep and try to get to the root of the problem so I could help him realize where his anxiety was coming from.

I asked for permission to coach him through what he was experiencing, and he agreed. As he told me about the disagreement he'd had with his girlfriend, I knew there was much more to it than that. I proceeded to ask him questions designed to help him cut through the layers of pain and anger he had inside. He opened up and said he had anger towards "his mom"; he also expressed how much stress he had gone through as a kid. He told me how many nights he went to sleep crying because of the yelling, and how he had laid there, hoping Mom would just come into the room and hug him. As I listened to this my heart was breaking—I was the root cause of his anxiety!—but I couldn't think about that. I had to be strong for him and continue wearing my "coaching hat," helping him have a breakthrough in a very difficult situation.

When he was finished speaking, I asked him what he needed from his mom in order to put things behind him. Still crying, he said he just wanted to be validated. He then made a very astute observation of his own behavior. During the disagreement with his girlfriend he had been looking for validation, which she never gave him. This lack of validation took him back to a place in his childhood that he didn't like, thus triggering his anxiety.

After hearing him out and getting him to realize where the root of his anxiety was coming from, I then switched back to my mom hat and hugged him. I cried with him and asked for forgiveness. I knew I couldn't change the past, but I had also learned that my life is not defined by my past or even my worst mistakes. What I could do now was offer him a better future. It had turned out to be a breakthrough moment for both of us.

The fact is, kids pick up on our energy and stress, no matter how hard we try to hide it. It also affects them more than we think. As with adults, kids' stress comes from outside sources, for example, hearing Mom and Dad argue while they are lying in bed trying to fall asleep, listening to them discuss work troubles, or falling victim to their bad moods. They also get stressed from worrying about a relative's illness; anticipating a doctor's visit; being picked on by a sibling; or just having a bad day at school.

As parents we should be very mindful how we discuss these issues when the kids are near because children will pick up on our anxieties and start to worry themselves. It is important to encourage our kids to be open and teach them to express what they are feeling and why they are feeling it. Expressing interest in their feelings shows your kids that they are important to you. Remember that some level of stress is normal; Let your kids know that it is okay to feel angry, scared, lonely, or anxious, and that other people share those feelings. Give them reassurance and let them know you understand they are stressed. Never dismiss their feelings as inappropriate.

Another thing I have learned through personal and professional experience is that people who fail to develop a strong sense of self tend to have weak boundaries. They want to be and do what everyone else expects of them; they also expect others to fill their needs and oftentimes blame them when those needs aren't met. This can extend to, and negatively affect, their children.

By developing a sense of self, you build the ability to self-regulate and better manage your anxiety, which brings about changes that allow you to be less reactive to stressful situations. It also means your need for everything to go smoothly decreases, as do your expectations and feelings of distress. Feeling less stressed is all about learning to manage your own part in your relationships with others, instead of trying to manage their feelings and anxiety. Therefore, I encourage my clients to dig deep to examine what causes them stress and how they manage it.

It is important to pay attention to your body, mind, and emotions, especially when feeling stressed out. You're responsible only for yourself, so be kind to yourself. Don't neglect your true views out of fear that someone else will have a different opinion. When a difficult situation arises and anxiety is high, avoiding the issue and distancing yourself isn't particularly helpful. Work on being who you want to be, even when you're around people who have different opinions or make annoying remarks; that includes responding in ways that are suitable for you and beneficial to your functioning and health. A good place to start is by taking a few deep breaths, as this brings in the rational mind and reduces your anxiety around stressful situations.

Sometimes just acknowledging that you're annoyed is enough to give you room to deal with the frustration and anger. Remember, validating your own feelings is key to developing a strong sense of self and will make dealing with the stressful situation much easier. As you change, you will relieve any burden you've placed on others in your life, including your children, and provide them with a strong role model for setting boundaries and self-care.

Chapter 5
Identifying and Reducing Stress Caused by Financial Challenges

W e've all been there. Money gets tight, debts rise and so does your stress level. Despite your best efforts to remain cool, calm, and collected, you find yourself snapping at your spouse or your kids and spacing out at work wondering how you're going to juggle it all.

Take a deep breath. The financial challenges you're facing can be better handled with a clear focus and a calm mind. That stress isn't helping and, in many cases, it may be holding you back from moving forward because it has you trapped like a deer in headlights.

Unlike other stress, financial overwhelm is easy to identify. It is staring us in the face every time we get the mail or look at our bank balance. While we can certainly look at the root causes of abundance issues, my coaching around this topic is primarily designed to help you take action to fix it.

As seen with Bob in a previous chapter, a lot of the stress in men comes from the fear of not being able to provide for their family.

Alex, for example, was very clear when he called me for a consultation. "I need help managing my finances," he said, "I don't know where to begin but I have debt that I need to clear up and I want to fix my credit." During our first session I learned more about Alex's situation. Alex, who was married with a young daughter, had a well-paid job. They were living with a family member and were not paying rent, just contributing as needed with food and other household expenses. His wife also worked, and they had no other bills, yet they had no money saved. Alex didn't know what he was doing wrong; what he did know was that his life, outlook, and loved ones were being negatively impacted by financial stress. Alex was in a sinking boat and did not know how to get out.

I began by asking him a series of questions, the first of which was why he had decided to do this now. He stated that he wanted to buy a house to provide a better future for his family; it also bothered him deeply that he had nothing to show for all his hard work. He admitted that his credit was poor, then revealed that he didn't trust the banks and kept whatever money he did have in a safe at home. I asked Alex what his timeline was for wanting to accomplish some financial stability.

"Two years," he replied, "In two years I want to be in my own house."

"Okay," I said, "We can do this. I will help you reach your goal as long as you are putting forth the effort and I will hold you accountable for your actions through this process."

He readily agreed.

I then asked him the following questions, which you can also ask yourself when trying to assess whether you're dealing with excessively high financial stress levels:

- Are you arguing with your spouse and family members more often? Are these fights money-related?
- Are you having headaches or panic attacks?
- Are you hiding bills and receipts from your spouse so you don't "get caught" spending money?
- Are you having difficulty falling asleep or staying asleep at night?
- Are you stress eating (i.e. turning to comfort and junk foods)?
- Are you having trouble focusing at work?

If you answered yes to any of these questions, then financial stress may be impacting your life more than you think.

Alex answered yes to most of these questions, which helped me gauge the level of assistance he needed. I then moved on to the next step, which was to create a budget sheet for him. When faced with financial stress, you need to do things to deal with the cause of the stress, as well as the resulting symptoms that the stress is creating in your life. In fact, addressing the symptoms is often the first thing to do because the physical and emotional strain you feel can make it harder to make clear-headed key decisions that need to be made later in the process.

"Just Breathe. You are strong enough to handle your challenges, wise enough to find a solution to your problems, and capable enough to do whatever needs to be done."
~ *Lori Deschene*

"Okay, Alex," I said, "now it's time to get real with your finances." I grabbed a piece of paper and wrote his net pay at the top. I then organized his challenges into categories: bills, gas, food, miscellaneous, et cetera, and provided him with steps he could take to begin lifting some of that emotional and mental burden off his shoulders. Indeed, financial stress is often alleviated by taking action. For example, if your mortgage is underwater, or your interest rate is too high for what the market has to offer, this may be a good time to look into refinancing. Even if you don't know the solution yet, just knowing there's a solution out there and that it's something you should pursue is a first step.

You must also look at other factors that are exacerbating your stress. Some are contributing factors to your current situation, for example, divorce, a bad economy, ongoing medical or health challenges, or changes in your career or job. These are all big things in life that definitely affect your outlook, but you often cannot do anything about. You must simply find ways to cope. Other things are not that important but rather annoyances that nonetheless add to your stress level. These you need to let go. Maybe your parents never taught you how to budget properly or they didn't teach you how to use credit properly. It doesn't matter. You cannot change what happened or did not happen in the past; however, you can do better for yourself.

Alex did the right thing by seeking coaching to address the emotional burden, as were other men who have come to me with financial stress and difficulty managing their money. Two of them were on the verge of losing their marriages, and another was a young guy who had ruined his credit due to poor money management. This problem is quite common, but with some tools and budgeting, you can turn the situation around, and attain some piece of mind in the process.

Getting things off your chest is often the easiest way to reduce stress and start feeling better. Keeping your financial stress a secret or internalizing it is a good way to wind up with an ulcer. I speak from personal experience when I say that. Let it out. Talk to a family member, friend, life coach, or a professional therapist to start venting that pressure so it doesn't build up and paralyze you.

After our second session, Alex told me he felt like he could breathe easier. I reminded him that although we were creating a financial plan, he wasn't out of the woods yet. It was important to keep up with the solutions we had identified and put in place, even if they were tough. I reminded him that cutting back may be difficult, but he'd rather be a little bored and not bothered by stress than entertained by some expensive distraction he would regret later.

I am happy to say that less than two years later Alex was debt-free; his credit was excellent, and he had purchased his first home. He took the necessary steps, put effort and made sacrifices to make this happen. He is now saving money to go on a vacation with his family. The other client with whom I used this same strategy paid off all his credit cards, increased his credit score, fixed his rocky relationship with his wife (a lot of their arguments were over finances), and is now working on his retirement plan.

People often fall into bad habits when they get extremely stressed. I am immensely proud of my clients for identifying those bad habits, addressing them, and changing the behavior.

Realize that no stress or burden lasts forever. Many times, stress is generated by the fear that we've ruined our financial lives, but that's usually not the case. Even if you lose your home to foreclosure and have to declare bankruptcy, the damage to your credit will only last for seven to ten years, and the impact starts to reduce long before that. You can recover and you will be able to get back to where you want to be. It just takes patience and a clear path forward!

Following this path requires us to accept that change is a part of life. Even significant changes that seem like the end of your world are just the start of something different. Losing your high-paying job or moving back in with your parents may feel like failure but going back to where you came from could reignite a passion you've lost and give you a new career path. Let go and find fulfillment in exploring new opportunities.

Be thankful. Take comfort in what you have. We often spend too much time focused on what we're lacking or missing from our lives instead of counting our blessings. Find the good in each day and focus on that as you continue to take one step at a time toward financial stability.

Take time to recharge. At least once a day, do something—anything—that will take your mind off your finances for a few minutes. Take your kids to the park to play, get out in your yard to garden for a while, or take a walk with a friend. Just getting away and letting yourself relax a little will actually make you more focused when you need to really get down to work on overcoming whatever financial challenges you face.

Chapter 6
Emotional Stress

H ave you ever felt like your emotions are having you, rather than the other way around? Many of us experience unpredictable mood swings that seem to affect every area of our lives. This chapter will give you tools to identify, manage, and express your emotions in a more controlled way.

Emotional stress can be particularly painful and challenging to deal with; it can also take more of a toll than many other forms of stress because thinking about and/or discussing potential solutions can be stressful in and of itself. Healthy coping strategies, therefore, include those that redirect you away from rumination and avoidance and toward emotionally proactive approaches, such as meditation.

If you're finding it difficult to manage your emotional stress, you are not alone. I wasn't always good at it and have dealt with my fair share of health issues as a result. Now I host Stress Management workshops to teach others about the dynamics of stress and the role it plays in our lives. For example, a certain amount of stress can be a good thing. It helps us work harder and faster in spurts, meaning we can perform at our best when we need to. It is the ongoing, unchecked stress that causes a host of physical and mental health conditions.

> *"The greatest weapon against stress is our ability to choose one thought over another."*
> *~ William James*

This was the issue for Amanda, who reached out to me via email after hearing about my workshops. Apparently, a well-meaning co-worker had attended the workshop and gave her one of the handouts I provide. The handout contained tools we can use on our own to manage stress better, but by that point Amanda was completely overwhelmed and felt she needed one-on-one help. She was walking around with a heart monitor because of irregular heart rhythm, palpitations, shortness of breath and tightness in her chest—all signs of acute stress. She also told me she had no desire to do anything because she didn't want to ruin anyone else's day with her stress.

For example, one of her favorite things to do was entertaining at her house, but she was so focused on trying to make everything perfect that she couldn't enjoy herself. We discussed some of the tools she could use to manage this stress, including letting go of details she had no control over. You'll notice that I mention the need to let go throughout this book, but it bears repeating. It is one of the first, and most important, steps to effective stress management.

Amanda was excited and highly motivated to put these tools to practice. Over the next few weeks, I watched her transform; she was happy and carried herself with more confidence. She planned a get-together at her house and later told me that her friends and family had noticed the difference and asked her what she had done to bring it about. Amanda had done an incredible job of recognizing her stress and working on finding positive ways and strategies for managing it better.

Causes of Emotional Stress

Our relationships greatly impact our lives, for better or for worse. Healthy relationships not only bring good times, but resources in times of need and added resilience in times of stress. They can even increase longevity. However, conflicted relationships and "frenemies" can take a heavy toll on us, both emotionally and physically.

There are a host of other factors that cause emotional stress, for example, financial crises or an unpleasant work environment; however, a key characteristic is a feeling of hopelessness. It is this feeling that sometimes leads us to unhealthy coping behaviors that only make matters worse. If we cannot change our stress levels by eliminating the stressful situation, we can still work on our emotional response to it.

When we feel emotional stress it's also often experienced as physical pain: a "heavy" feeling in the chest, an unsettled feeling in the stomach, a dull headache. It's common to try to escape these feelings, but it can actually be helpful to go deeper into the experience and take note of what our body is trying to tell us. Some people notice that the pain seems more intense for a while then begins to dissipate as the emotion lessens. What happens when you try it?

If you find yourself constantly battling an urge to obsess, allow yourself a limited amount of time to think about your situation fully and mull over solutions, come up with hypothetical possibilities, and replay upsetting exchanges. Fully immerse yourself, but then give yourself permission to move on and try some healthy distractions. This allows you to take a break from rumination by actively redirecting your thoughts; it also provides practice in choosing your thoughts which can help eliminate some emotional stress in the long term. You may find yourself more relaxed the rest of the day because you know that you have "permission" to focus for a time on your emotional situation; that time is just later.

In the past, many therapists and coaches counseled their client to express every emotion they felt (or at least the big ones), the rationale being that if they did not these emotions would show themselves in other ways. Yes, it is true that "stuffing" our emotions can be unhealthy and that there are benefits to examining them to discern what lessons they have for us; however, it has also been discovered that distracting oneself from emotional pain with healthy alternatives such as a feel-good movie, fun activities with friends, or a hobby can help us reduce stress and feel better.

When you find yourself mentally or verbally complaining about something, do something to change your emotional pattern. One way to do this is to rethink your assumptions. Are you assuming something is a negative event when that might not necessarily be the case? For example, having your plans cancelled at the last minute can be seen as a negative, or you may see it as extra time you now have to do something productive.

Whatever the cause of your emotional stress,

you can work toward lessening and managing it without losing the "messages" your emotions are giving you.

Our lives are primarily defined, not by our abilities, talents, or actions, but by the emotions we feel on a daily basis. Our emotions are like the ocean—some days they're a brewing storm, other days they're calm as can be. It is therefore important for us to take control of them as much as possible, particularly in times of stress. When we start to recognize each emotion and its connection to the circumstances in our lives, we can utilize them to change the quality of our experience.

Emotions are signals calling us to action. Often-times, the painful emotions are powerful indicators that we need to make changes.

Like stress, our emotions are determined by the rules we set and the meanings, interpretations, or perceptions we attach to them. In other words, what we feel is not based on our experience but on our interpretation of that experience.

The next time you find yourself stressing about something or deciding you're not up to a challenge, stop and rethink; see if you can come up with a neutral or positive replacement. Do not make that "negative" event a stressor in your life, because it does not have to be. It comes down to what we focus on. We have to learn how to let go of what we have no control over and focus on what is in our control. While external factors can create a negative environment and impact how we feel, we ultimately have the power to control our own emotions and our moods. It's important to avoid triggers that create negative energy and work towards getting over the hurdles quickly in order to get back to a happier state. People's behaviors manifest out of insecurities, fears, and anger. Remember that nobody can make you unhappy without your permission. Of all the things I consistently tell my clients, this is one I cannot stress enough.

Also, remember the practice of transformational vocabulary discussed in an earlier chapter. Consciously selecting the words you use to describe your feelings, both to yourself and others, can change your mood faster than anything else. In essence, it is a type of personal reflection that can smooth out life's bumps, boost our happiness, and help us become the people we want to be.

Chapter 7
How Our Stress Affects Others in Our Lives

S tress and feeling stressed out are highly conta-
gious, so by taking time to recharge regularly
we can have calm energy that helps others
around us calm down too.

Have you ever found yourself in a situation where
your to-do list seems endless, deadlines are fast ap-
proaching, and you want to scream at the top of your
lungs? Of course, you have, and it's not a pleasant
feeling, but have you ever given much thought to
what stress really is and how it affects us?

Stress is not necessarily a "bad" thing. In fact,
without it humankind would not have survived. It
is our inherent fight or flight response that prepared
our ancestors to escape or defeat physical danger.

> *"It's not the stress that kills us, it's our reaction
> to it." ~ Hans Selye*

The challenge is when our body goes into a state

of stress in inappropriate situations. When blood flow is going only to the most vital muscles needed to fight or flee, brain function is minimized. We may feel agitated or aggressive, which is helpful when dealing with predators but not so much when dealing with family, friends, or co-workers. This is the "fight" reaction.

Some of us avoid our stress by removing ourselves from the situation instead of tackling it. This "flight" can actually escalate and prolong the conflict, which brings us stress.

Still other people might "freeze" when stressed, which sets the stage for a poor emotional response. The energy caused by the perceived threat gets "locked" into the nervous system, hence the freeze. This response sometimes reveals itself when we breathe (i.e. holding our breath or breathing shallowly). The occasional deep sigh is the nervous system catching up on its oxygen intake. Then there are the relatively few people who, no matter how severe the stress, have a tendency to roll with it. They see a molehill where someone else seems a mountain.

As mentioned in the chapter on kids and stress, how we react to stress affects others in our lives. We also learned that a stressful environment can affect us even if we're not the ones directly experiencing the stress. If we want those around us to be stress-free, we don't do this by managing their emotions; we do it by managing ours.

Unchecked stress also wreaks havoc on your relationships. Think of those times you came home after a particularly tough day at work. You are full of pent-up stress and cannot resist unloading on your partner/roommate/friend/parent/sibling. A bit of venting is okay, however, when you are not only taking home stress but taking it out on others, it can damage the relationship.

Think of it this way: people who are always complaining about being stressed can come off as self-centered. The moment you start to think things are worse for you than for others is the moment you start alienating yourself from them.

When trying to figure out the areas in which you most commonly get stuck, I find it helpful to consider these two questions:

- Are you dealing with your feelings, or the feelings of those around you?
- Is every decision you make determined by your intention to manage your feelings in one way or another (i.e. to either feel better or to avoid feeling bad)?

These are among the things I thought about during my turbulent years, when my life consisted of vicious cycles of heartache, stress, betrayal, depression, anxiety...basically, every negative feeling you can imagine. Storm after storm kept coming and I was losing the hope of ever seeing the sunshine again. Then, shortly after I divorced my husband, the thoughts began.

You should write a book.

For a while I ignored this voice in my head, saying, "There's nothing that I could say that other authors couldn't say better!"

Have you ever felt that way? Torn between the desire to do something and the belief that you weren't qualified to do it?

One day, while I was in my room crying, I suddenly began to imagine my life differently. I said to myself, *I want to see you smile; You can do it; You are resilient.* That's when I realized I could choose to change my life; I also realized that my stress was not just affecting me but others in my life as well. If I gave myself over to despair, what sort of example was I setting for my children and everyone else around me?

Then I heard a voice inside say, *You can smile—even through your tears.* That was a turning point for me. I began to journal, putting all my thoughts, feelings, and emotions on paper. This thought gave me new hope and new inspiration for the book I had always wanted to write.

I began seeing all the trauma and heartache I had experienced not as obstacles, but as opportunities.

Each day, I noted the many choices I had—the choice to smile through my tears and to inspire others going through similar hardships. They were chances for me to look at the worst that life had to offer square in the eyes, face my fears, and refuse to be defeated. To refuse to fall into despair.

Life could change in an instant. Everything you think is so important could vanish, or least appear to. The only thing of permanence is your gift of love, because when you give it you are guaranteed to feel it, whether the other people return it or not.

When people have been struggling with a problem for many years, they often are hard on themselves about it. It's important to realize that blaming yourself doesn't solve anything; it only makes thinks worse. If you can understand the positive behind your problem, you can understand how to change it in the most effective way. You can also change the behavior by identifying what emotion triggers it. Then it's all about breathing and making a different choice.

One of the challenges I face when coaching is that people experience stress in so many different ways. I have found it seems to target us where we are weakest, physiologically and mentally.

For example, if you are prone to headaches, eczema, psoriasis, or inflammatory disorders, these will flare up in times of stress. If you have low levels of patience or tolerance for others, this will be the first area to present. For others, stress may lead to heart disease, hypertension, and high blood pressure; it can affect the immune system, and has been linked to strokes, IBS (Irritable Bowel Syndrome), ulcers, diabetes, muscle and joint pain, miscarriage, allergies, and much more. All stressed-out people exhibit changes; it may be emotional, physical, behavioral, or a combination of all three. The trick is to notice negative changes, keeping in mind that they are also likely to set off a chain of unpleasant or unhealthy events that will affect those around us.

Again, stress isn't avoidable, but the health risks it poses are. The key to minimizing the risk is to identify stress-related problems as early as possible so that action can be taken before serious stress-related illness occurs.

My own journey from stressed-out to stress management has led me to amazing things. I learned to access my feelings of gratitude and appreciation for what I have, as well as for my own positive intent. I had to learn to let go of things I had no control over, which for me was the hardest part. Once I learned to focus on what was working in my life rather than things I couldn't control, stress was no longer a negative force in my life. In fact, the management of stress became my passion. I began educating myself on topics related to stress, eventually obtained my certification as a Life Coach, and began to host workshops to help empower others. If I can learn to manage stress in positive ways, so can you.

Remember to love yourself. Embrace happiness. Pursue your dreams. You are in control of your own future and the people you choose to share your life with. You are secure in yourself and that is also a blessing. Don't let the actions of others change who you are deep down inside.

In addition to journaling, I recommend keeping a stress diary for a few weeks. It is a highly effective tool to help you become more aware of the situations that cause you to become stressed.

Note down the date, time, and place of each stressful episode, and note what you were doing, who you were with, and how you felt both physically and emotionally. Use the diary to understand what triggers your stress and how effective you are in stressful situations. This will enable you to avoid stressful situations and develop better coping mechanisms when such situations are unavoidable. Stress can be triggered by a problem that may on the surface seem impossible to solve. Learning how to find solutions to your problems will help you feel more in control, thereby lowering your level of stress.

Another stress management tool you can use is the problem-solving technique. This involves writing down the problem and coming up with as many possible solutions as you can. Decide on the good and bad points of each one and select the best solution. Write down each step that you need to take as part of the solution: what will be done, how will it be done, when will it be done, who is involved and where will it take place. It also serves as a re-minder that you are in control of your own actions, decisions, and choices, and that you shouldn't enter into any situation or make any decisions that will later leave you feeling stressed.

Recall the exercise in a previous chapter regard-ing the physical manifestation of stress. I would like you to try that now. Think of a stressor in your life that you'd like to change or understand better. Now, as you hold it in your mind, touch the part of your body where you think that stress resides. What ignites that stress, and the accompanying emotions within you? Touch, and trust your intuition, your first gut reaction. Where does it go? Where does it come from?

While touching that body part, I want you to go within; I want you to understand that everything has a reason. Even though it may not look very pretty right now, this stress has a purpose, or what's called a "positive intent." The more you resist something, the more it continues. The more you fight something, the more it fights back so you just get caught up in that fight and nothing changes. By doing this exercise we learn to appreciate stress for what it can teach us; we also learn how to manage it so that it doesn't get the better of us.

When you can understand the reason or positive intent behind the stress you are faced with, you are trusting that it is there to serve you, even though it hurts at the moment. You are also taking responsibility for your own stress, so that it does not affect others in your life.

Chapter 8
Stress Management in the Workplace

Prominent psychologist and Berkeley professor Richard S. Lazarus defined stress as "a condition or feeling experienced when a person perceives that 'demands exceed the personal and social resources the individual is able to handle.'" Nowhere is this condition felt more than the modern workplace.

When I met Lisa, she was hanging by the end of her professional rope. Though she was a very hard worker, she felt undervalued and unappreciated. It seemed her co-workers were trying to push her out, by either pushing her buttons so she would quit or by trying to get her fired. Her superiors also undermined her, and her immediate boss had a dismissive attitude whenever she tried to talk about how she was feeling. In short, she felt that everyone was out to get her. It got so bad that she filed grievances with the HR department, stating that she was working in a hostile work environment. In the meantime, she had become very defensive, irritable, angry, frustrated, highly stressed and, eventually, physically ill. Soon she was taking anti-anxiety medication because the thought of going to work each morning was overwhelming. Lisa told me that even on her days off she was unable to relax because her mind was racing with thoughts of what she would have to deal with the next time she went in.

Lisa was so focused on what everyone else was doing to her that she never stopped to think about what she was doing to contribute to the stress she was feeling. After months of working with her, I was able to help her shift her focus from others' behavior to her own growth, shed limiting beliefs, and realize her worth. She also learned to control her emotions when she felt pushed. More importantly, she came to understand that her perception of her co-workers was actually of her own feelings about herself, and that this low-vibrational energy radiated out to everyone around her. In fact, she has even apologized to her co-workers for times when she misread or overreacted to them. Lisa is now a very successful person, so happy and full of life that she actually has a glow about her. She goes to work each day free of stress and with a smile on her face, all because she was able to shift her focus to what she wanted and how she wanted to feel.

Prolonged, unchecked stress prevents people from functioning at their best. **Stress is the biggest hindrance to productivity, efficiency, and even profitability.** It can lead to absenteeism, low morale, and increased staff turnover.

Common workplace stressors include:

- Low salaries
- Excessive workloads
- Few opportunities for growth or advancement
- Work that isn't engaging or challenging
- Lack of support
- Not having enough control over job-related decisions
- Conflicting demands or unclear performance expectations

Work-related stress is also one of the major factors in a variety of health conditions. As with any kind of stress, the body thinks it is under attack and switches to "fight or flight" mode, releasing a complex mix of hormones and chemicals to prepare the body for physical action. This causes a number of reactions, from blood being diverted to muscles to shutting down unnecessary bodily functions such as digestion.

Think of it this way: when a bridge has too heavy

a load on it and that load is left there long enough, it will eventually collapse. You would be able to see the warning signs before this happens; the bridge would bow, buckle, groan, and creak. The same principle can be applied to human beings—when excessive demands and challenges are placed on us, we too will ultimately collapse. That collapse might manifest as a nervous breakdown or serious health issues such as a heart attack or cancer. And, as in the case of the bridge, there would be early warning signs, such as mood swings, insomnia, repeated short-term absence, dips in productivity and efficiency, and weight loss/gain.

Some of the signs of collapse within the work environment include:

- Increased absenteeism
- Friction and even hostility between colleagues
- Gossip and negativity
- Work not being completed to a high standard
- Feeling constantly rushed and unable to concentrate
- Being unable to "switch off" from work
- Feeling tired all the time
- Dreading going to work
- Anxiety when at work
- Losing their sense of humor and becoming

moody and irritable
- Altering their working patterns (for example, staying late or refusing to take breaks)
- Taking more sick leave
- Increased accidents and mistakes
- Increased work conflict and grievances
- Damage to office reputation
- Damage to goodwill and motivation
- Increased liability for personal injury

Research indicates that organizations can improve employee well-being by identifying factors that will reduce employee stress and improve overall performance.

Effective stress management brings the following benefits:

- Reduced absences due to sickness
- Improved staff retention and ability to attract the best talent
- Increased motivation and higher performance
- Enhanced reputation as a business of choice
- Improve overall performance
- Team effort and collaboration on tasks
- Higher standards and morale in the office
- Positivity, encouragement, and collaboration among staff members

Stress management can help both staff and managers recognize the signs and symptoms of stress, to be able to define it, and introduce a variety of personal resilience techniques to best equip you with the tools to deal with increasing pressure and demands of the workplace. A healthy workplace is a more productive workplace!

"You cannot resolve a problem until you are aware that there is a problem."
~ Iyanla Vanzant

To create a resilient workforce, it's important for staff members to:

- Recognize the signs and symptoms of stress
- Understand the causes and effects of stress
- Learn practical techniques and strategies to deal with stress

Stress should be viewed as any other health and safety risk hazard. Therefore, employers should be assessing stress risks in a practical, consistent, and coherent way.

What can we do as a team to reduce stress? Here are some tools:

Take stress seriously! Tackling stress is part of health and safety responsibilities and employers are legally obligated to take action when someone reports such issues.

Communicate well. Keep staff informed about workplace changes. Be clear about job roles and targets and be sensitive in the way you communicate. Give timely and accurate feedback, as this improves employees' confidence and keeps them informed on areas to work on. This can provide a consistent approach to prevent an overload of criticisms, which can impact on stress levels.

Remember teamwork. Focus on creating good team spirit and get all staff involved and engaged. Organize company events outside the office, such as "well-being days." Being valued and involved like this is a major factor in happiness at work.

People often feel stressed when they are powerless over their job product. If change is required, consult those involved so they can have a say in work-related decisions.

Create Action Plans around work-related stress. They can include:

- Modifying existing support resources
- Creating or amending policies
- Organizing additional training
- Addressing leadership
- Meetings to communicate to staff expecta-

tions and objectives
- Changing management or protocols around time management issues
- Understanding an individual's perception of their stress-related challenges
- Finding ways to support the individual

Action Plans can be used as a proactive measure when an individual is showing early signs of stress to explore its causes and provide adequate support. They can also be helpful when communication between a staff member and their manager or higher authority has become strained. The key here is to let the staff member know that they are heard and understood.

How effective are your managers at managing stress?

A company's management team can contribute to reducing staff stress, but they may also be the cause of it. Management behavior is often highlighted as a major factor by those suffering from work-related stress. As the first line of support for general staff, managers play a key role in the identification and management of stress within the business. They will often be in the best position to notice changes in staff behavior that may indicate a stress-related problem; they will also often be the first point of contact when an individual feels stressed. Ensuring your managers are equipped to their best ability to deal with stress can generate a huge return and increase the productivity and efficiency of the workplace. Also, developing confidentiality protocols will help staff feel comfortable enough to address stress-related issues with management, leaders, and bosses.

Acknowledgment can be a powerful tool in business, both in terms of profitability and increasing employee satisfaction. If you're in management, ask yourself the best ways to build appreciation into your leadership routine. By taking the time to acknowledge each individual's ability to contribute to organizational success, you demonstrate your confidence in them, thereby reducing their feeling of "Nothing I do is ever good enough." Where there is an appreciation for a good job, there will most likely be more work efficiency and willingness among the employees.

As we saw in the case of Lisa, a dismissive attitude on the part of leadership can exacerbate a stressful situation. If you are in management, know this: being dismissive is one of the best ways to make sure people hate you. Your body language speaks volumes, so if you're looking away from people, checking your phone or interrupting them while they are speaking, you are telling them they are unimportant. When you dismiss people, you are also missing out on their ideas and talents. Oftentimes, managers are not aware they are doing this—they are juggling a million things and doing their best to meet their own demands. This is why any workplace stress management program should include some kind of "awareness" training so leaders can take note of their behavior and make the necessary positive adjustments.

Chapter 9
Gossip in the Workplace

Gossip can be an extremely destructive force and a major source of stress, so much so that I felt it deserved its own chapter. Let's return again to Lisa, who felt antagonized and undermined at work until she was able to shift her perspective. While we are all ultimately responsible for our emotions, backstabbing at the workplace is a common and very real problem. In fact, if we were to ask a roomful of people to describe what they hated most about places they had worked "gossip" would likely be at the top of the list. First, let's talk about why gossip happens. People wouldn't do it if it didn't serve a purpose, and in fact, gossip has three of them:

- It is a valued source of information for those who mistrust formal channels.
- It sometimes serves as an emotional release for anger or frustration.
- It is used as an indirect way of surfacing or engaging in interpersonal conflicts.

Gossip flourishes in an unhealthy social system. In a work setting, people engage in gossip when they lack trust or efficacy and turn to peers rather than leaders with whom they feel they cannot raise sensitive issues or grievances.

The problem with gossip is that it reinforces the sickness that generated it in the first place. When people traffic in gossip the real issues never get aired, therefore there is no opportunity to clear up any misconceptions. This leads to more speculation, thus the need for more gossip. As gossip is often malicious as well, it often causes a breakdown in relationships and becomes a self-fulfilling prophecy. Of course, it is also hurtful and a source of stress for the person(s) being targeted by the gossip.

The best way to stop gossip is to stop enabling it. Gossipers don't need anyone to agree with them; their reward is spreading the "news" to a willing audience. The listener, even a passive one, is still perpetuating the problem. Gossip must be forced out into the open, and those trafficking in it need to know that they risk being called out and held accountable for what they say. Leaders in the workplace can help reduce the need for and supply of gossip by creating a safe place to hold honest, open discussions rather than allowing grievances to metastasize. They can also try to come up with ways to challenge employees/co-workers to use their skills to create the values they want rather than gossiping and backbiting. Remember, gossip is a symptom of a deeper problem, and when leaders create trust through healthy communication and transparency, the need for rumors and speculation disappears.

If someone at your job starts to spread gossip, don't waste your valuable time listening. Instead, be upfront with that person by saying something like, "This is not something I want to hear or talk about," or "Just because someone said it doesn't make it true." That said, if something you hear is concerning to you or the business, you may feel the need to verify; just be sure to use discretion and never act on rumors. Remember, there are always two sides to every story, and the less we say about others the better off we are. In fact, refusing to participate in spreading gossip and rumors increases our chances of being trusted and becoming a leader.

Workplaces assume employees have sufficient communication skills because they went to school and were taught these skills; however, this is often not so. Most people struggle with verbal and written communication, and when you add ethnic diversity, various dialects, and regional differences in com-munication to the mix, the potential for misunder-standing multiplies. Communication basics, such as active listening and being assertive, should be mandatory training for all staff members, including management. Like everyone else, bosses' personal experience and beliefs around disagreements strongly influence their responses to workplace situations, and unfortunately, this response can include yelling, storming out, shutting down, using positional power, talking down to others, and/or swearing at them. Others might take the passive aggressive approach and pretend everything is okay, only to undermine the employee later. None of these strategies demonstrate healthy communication skills, and they certainly don't increase the likelihood of resolution. Instead, they escalate employees' fear of having difficult conversations and increasing stress in the workplace. Part of building a healthy environment is to set communication guidelines so employees know what to expect when they sit down to discuss a difference of opinion with a co-worker or manager.

We all want to be heard. It's gratifying, empowering, and makes us feel valued. When we are having a difference of opinion, we want our perspective to be validated. We want others to get who we are and to hear our arguments, even if they don't agree with us.

Have you ever dined in a restaurant that has

a swinging door in and out of the kitchen? Ever pushed (or watched someone push) on that door when another body is trying to get through from the other direction? What happens? You push, they push, and nobody gets through.

The same push-pushback phenomenon occurs when two people want to get their differing viewpoints across at the same time. It usually sounds something like:

"Yes, but you're wrong because..." or "No, you weren't listening. What I am trying to say is..." and so on, and before you know it, you're at an impasse.

That said, getting a point across should not be your goal when trying to resolve a conflict, be it at work, home, with friends, et cetera. Your goal should be to understand their views and their perception of things.

We can't forget that everything we experience is filtered through our own perception.

I learned this firsthand when I had issues with others at my own job. It was a hostile work environment, or so I thought. I am not saying that such environments do not exist, but in my case, much like Lisa's, it was all about how I was perceiving things. My co-worker had her own perception of things—she thought I had it out for her and wanted to get her fired. Now, when I look back at the situation I can see that we were both pushing so hard to be heard that neither one of us was listening to the other or taking the time to understand the other's feelings. It was only after I put the tools in this book into practice that things improved.

Stress in the workplace does exist, but we can learn to manage it in healthy and positive ways.

Ways You Can Manage Your Workplace Stress

As mentioned many times throughout this book, your stress level is determined by your perspective and how you process things. No one, not even toxic co-workers or managers, can create stress within you; only you do that, just as you are the only one who can change it. Your greatest challenge is your fear of that change. This is why so many people stay in jobs that make them miserable. It is when you start to look fear in the face that you gain strength, courage, and confidence with every experience. Remember, once fear is acted upon the death of fear is certain.

- Track your stressors. Keep a journal for a week or two to identify which situations create the most stress and how you respond to them. This practice will help you find patterns, which will make it easier for you to break them and make more empowering choices. My job involves a lot of typing, so when something bothers me or stresses me out, I type it out as a way to release it, delete it, and let it go. You can develop your own healthy responses when you feel the tension rising. Any form of physical activity is beneficial.

- Take time to recharge. To avoid the negative effects of chronic stress and burnout, we need time to reload and return to our pre-stress level of functioning. This recovery process requires "switching off" from work by having periods of time when you are neither engaging in work-related activities nor thinking about work. People have different preferences when it comes to how much they blend their work and home lives; regardless, everyone needs to establish some clear work-life boundaries in order to reduce the potential for work-life conflict and the stress that goes with it. When you take time off to relax and unwind, you come back to work feeling reinvigorated and ready to perform at your best.

- Remember that perfection does not exist, and you certainly don't have to know how to do things perfectly the first time around. When

you feel that pressure to be perfect, change that thought to a positive affirmation, such as "I know that I am doing the very best I can."
- Don't focus on who let you down at work; instead, appreciate those who lift you up.

You can't always avoid the tensions that occur on the job, yet you can take these steps to manage work-related stress. A positive outlook in life can go a long way.

Chapter 10
Relationship Stress

A deadlock in a relationship takes place when one partner makes a request and is repeatedly denied. The partner making the request asks again in a more forceful, controlling, or indirect way, while the other continues to resist and withhold, until all giving and receiving in the relationship becomes an implicit battle for control. The basis of a healthy relationship is the feeling that needs are met and shared. Every time a partner's needs are disrespected, resisted, or ignored the relationship deteriorates. Every time a partner does something to selfishly gain control, both partners lose confidence that their needs can be shared.

I've seen many couples whose relationships have lost their vitality and connectedness. Usually their sense of passionate engagement has gradually diminished over time; they've also missed many opportunities to do something about it because it felt too hard or painful.

Too many couples become motivated to get

their relationship back on track only after something traumatic happens. Let's say, for example, that one of them has an affair. After years of avoiding their problems, they suddenly enter panic mode. They decide that maybe it's time to try couples' therapy or relationship coaching. Unfortunately, they may find it is too late for them to reconnect to the attraction and love they once felt. The tragedy is that most people who end up at that place deeply regret having let things go so far. They did not realize how much they loved their spouse until it was too late to get them back.

This was the case in my marriage, though I did not want to admit it at the time. In the past, I operated under the assumption that a good marriage was invulnerable to infidelity, betrayal, or deception. After my divorce, I learned that this is not the case. I wish I knew back then what I know now, but I also know that everything happens for a reason—that all my struggles, traumas, and lessons all happened for me, not to me. It changed me for the better. I had to go through those lessons in order to be where I am today. I now know that even a loving, supportive, happy marriage can have a spouse who is less than confident in him or herself. I recognize that love is an action verb and that in order to feel that love I must first live it every day. I know now that love is the priority, above all of life's stress, annoyances, and grievances. A key component to living that love and also feeling less stressed is communication. No matter how much you love someone and how in sync you are, neither of you are mind readers. You must speak your thoughts, your fears, and your joys, because all of it matters and all must be shared if true intimacy is to be achieved and maintained.

There was a point in my life when I let stress get the best of me, and it affected my relationship with my spouse, my family, and my kids. I was feeling like I was at the edge of what I could handle, and since I lacked healthy coping skills my stress continued to build until I reached the point of no return. I felt all my hopes had been shattered.

When you let too much resentment accumulate, you are eventually left with bitterness, anger, frustration, anxiety, and depression, all of which lead to high levels of stress. By that time you likely have few positive feelings left for your partner, or perhaps no feelings at all. If you do wait until this stage to seek coaching or therapy, you may find that the only thing to do is admit how little you have left to save. There is no roadmap to heal from the demise of a relationship, just like there is no manual on parenting. Breakups, no matter how amicable, will come with pain and stress, but they also open a door to a new, better life. As a result of my experience, I realized that even I, someone everyone thought of as the ultimate multitasker and super mom, is not perfect. I had to give myself a break. This was a critical learning experience for me with regard to managing my stress.

Oftentimes, one partner sees things deteriorating and tries to take action; for example, they suggest talking more or having more sex or going go into counseling, but the other doesn't take them seriously. They do not want to acknowledge there is a problem, or they don't see why the relationship should require any effort. They may subscribe to the idea that relationships should just happen, without action or reflection. If their pleas go unheard long enough, the first partner's sadness and frustration will turn to resentment and grief. Their desires drop away. Their requests are replaced by silence.

This can happen over many months or years; either way it may well mark the point of no return. Suddenly, the person who had refused to acknowledge the problem feels a frightening shift in his/her partner; in other words, they no longer "nag" or care enough to be openly distressed. He or she may not even be around that much anymore, and they've certainly stopped planning for the future and suggesting family activities. This was the case when I had the privilege of coaching a young couple, Gina and Matt, who came to me for help because one of them felt checked out and the other was tired of trying to make it work. Both were under stress because they had withdrawn emotionally from the relationship due to years of betrayal and not feeling validated and appreciated by the other.

In session, as they sat side by side on the couch, I witnessed Gina raising an eyebrow at Matt's panicked tone. Gina was surprised that after withdrawing for all this time Matt suddenly seemed to care what was happening to the marriage. As mentioned earlier, sometimes it is too late. The relationship had been shattered and Gina who had tried for so long to keep it together now has only one thing to say: "I'm leaving."

It does not have to be this way; however, both partners have to have the courage to be honest and to take positive action, even when it's uncomfortable:

"In a relationship, when communication starts to fade, everything else follows."
~ Unknown

If you start to lose vitality in your relationship, if you feel resentment and a growing disconnect, that is the time to take real action together. When your deepest fears and insecurities rise to the surface, making it even more difficult to give yourself completely to another, that's the time for greater engagement with life and with each other. To be truly vulnerable with another, you must open up; however, many people find that terrifying, so rather than diving right in and swimming in the deep end, they live their lives on the surface, which is what Gina and Matt did for years.

The truth is your relationship stems directly from where you are. It's easy to be distracted and to blame our partners or external events for the state of the union. But if you want to create real, lasting change in your relationship and achieve a level of intimacy, passion, and connection that you've always dreamed about, you have to first look within. It starts with you being willing to let go of stress and step into your pain.

Stepping into your pain means facing your fears or stressors head-on. It means immersing yourself in them, rather than avoiding or even denying them altogether, as most of us tend to do. Yes, it sounds intimidating, and surely you could think of a thousand things you'd rather do. But by making the decision to face your pain, you are also making the decision to liberate yourself and create a new life.

It takes real courage to face your innermost challenges and to be absolutely vulnerable with your partner. But when you take the leap, you will be able grow in ways that you never have before. And, ultimately, you will learn how to connect with yourself and with your partner on an even deeper and more meaningful level. You do this by making a total commitment to the truth. You have to be willing to be open-minded and open-hearted, because this is the only path toward opening up a new sense of awareness.

The truth isn't always easy—it's not easy to handle and it's not always easy to find because a lot of us hide it from ourselves. However, it's in that moment of recognizing "I am scared" and then making the decision to follow that fear—that is how real change is made.

For most people, one of the greatest fears is following their fears! It's easier to pull back than to dive in. For Gina and Matt, the first step toward healing was to acknowledge their fears, their insecurities, their pain, and their stress. By doing this they created a new sense of awareness and honesty. This placed them in a better position to view their life from an even healthier and more objective perspective.

Once you have made a decision to commit to yourself and to the truth, you must understand that there are two deep-seated fears that every single human shares. First, there is the fear that they are not enough. Second, there is the fear that they will not be loved. Everyone, no matter how confident they are, no matter if they are the President of the United States or the greatest athlete in the world, has these two fears.

What challenges have these fears presented for you in your relationship? Perhaps you shut down in the midst of conflict or run from turmoil. Do you lash out when you feel scared? What are the times you feel alone? Understanding these fundamental fears can help you become more aware when stress enters your life or where your pain and insecurities stem from. You will be able to see just why you are holding back.

Oftentimes, we try to preserve an identity or cling so desperately to rules that we have constructed. We do that because we are scared of life outside those boundaries. Take the time to analyze and assess and become really curious about why we construct these walls and start knocking them down. By doing so you are going to discover the real you and see how you have been selling yourself short all this time. You are going to see how you are creating the relationship you are in. You will see how it is entirely within your power to create an extraordinary, magnificent relationship.

So, harness your courage, make this decision and take the leap. You will learn what it really is to be vulnerable. And you will see what it is to truly experience intimacy with a partner. To be free and liberated. To be yourself. To manage stress better and not sweat the little things. At the end of the day, isn't that what we all yearn for?

Remember to love yourself. Embrace happiness. Pursue your dreams. You are in control of your own future and the people you choose to share your life with. Become secure in yourself because that is also a blessing. Do not let his/her actions change who you are deep down inside. Yes, they should open your eyes and force you to look deeply at what weaknesses lay within you and your relationship, but do not allow them to change your soul.

Every day is a blessing, even those days that feel like a nightmare. You realize this when you look around and see how fragile life can be. Life continues regardless of the pain you feel and the tears you cry. Remember the sun rises each morning out of darkness and so shall you. When you place your feet upon the ground, connect yourself to the world and engage your mind, body, and soul in all that you do. Listen to your heart.

Chapter 11
Additional Tools for Handling Stress

Everyone is different, so are the ways they choose to manage their stress. For example, some people prefer pursuing hobbies such as gardening, playing music, dancing, painting, or playing sports, while others find relief in more solitary activities like meditation, yoga, walking, journaling or reading.

Throughout this book I have provided tools I have given my clients, with proven success. Below, I recap the most important ones and have added other ways in which you can alleviate your stress. While not every tool here will work for you, I suggest giving them a try and use the ones that do work as an everyday reminder that stress doesn't have to be a bad or a negative thing as long as we know how to manage it.

I. Transformational Vocabulary

As mentioned earlier, this is the conscious decision to choose words that positively describe a situation or person. This may feel inauthentic at first but try it anyway. With practice, you will find that you will start to believe what you are saying, just as you believed the negative verbiage you tell yourself. This is the time to practice positive verbiage. This will decrease stress and lift your mood. It will also change the way others respond to you, which in turn will yield the type of positive interactions you desire.

II. Identifying Your Emotions

Our emotions are signals and calls for actions.

Here are some common emotions and the messages they are likely trying to convey:

1. Uncomfortable: Clarify what you want and take action in that direction. Change your state. Now is a good time to expose the story you keep telling yourself why it's not possible or why it's too risky to start working on what it is you want to do.

2. Fearful: Get ready to do something. Change your perception about fear and instead of running away from it, embrace it, cherish it,

and talk to it. Figure out the story behind it and the lessons it holds for you.

3. Hurt: An expectation is not being met and you have a feeling of loss. Change your way of communicating your needs. Negative thoughts can fester in a person's mind like open wounds, and the quickest way to get rid of them is to change them into positive thoughts. When you find yourself thinking negatively of a person or situation, try to seek out the silver lining. Look for the good in that person or situation and focus on that.

4. Angry: An important rule has been violated. Someone once said, "Holding onto anger is like drinking poison and expecting the other person to die." Anger destroys happiness and letting go of anger and resentment is key to living a happy life. Let the person know that your standard may not be the same as theirs, talk about it, and let it go.

5. Frustrated: You need to change your approach to achieve your goal. Whenever you are feeling frustrated, this indicates that you are being held back from something by self-imposed barriers and limitations. Recognize the sources that trigger that feeling and use proper

techniques to choose a different emotional response. On the surface frustration feels uncomfortable, below the surface it can be quite beneficial and serve as an instant motivator that stimulates your imagination. Don't forget that everyone is on a separate path.

6. Disappointed: Your expectation may not be appropriate for the situation at hand. Being mindful of this feeling will help you capture the precise moment of disappointment. If you were not happy with yesterday, try something different today. Don't stay stuck, you can do better.

7. Guilty or Regretful: You violated one of your standards. A sense of responsibility for the actions taken. Feeling this after a mistake can lead to change. You must ensure you don't violate it again.

8. Inadequate: You need to improve what you are doing; your rules may be too hard to meet. You can heal yourself with the simple process of letting go of negative thoughts.

9. Overloaded, overwhelmed, hopeless, or depressed: You need to prioritize. List the things you want to accomplish in order of importance, then take action with the first item on

your list.

10. Lonely: You need connection with people. Surround yourself with people who will encourage you and can see your dreams and support them. We are all a product of our surroundings. If you choose to associate with positive people, their optimism and positivity will wear off on you. If you choose to associate with negative people, though, their anger and resentment will inevitably wear off on you as well.

"You are the average of the five people you spend the most time with"
~ Jim Rohn

III. Mastering Your Emotions

Once you learn what your emotions are telling you, you can manage those emotions, which will help you manage your stress and master your life better.

1. Identify: Once you have identified the emotion, you can appreciate the message. It is saying you must change something.

2. Clarify: What message is it offering? Do I need to change my perception (the meaning)

or my procedures (my communication or my behavior)?

3. Get curious and ask questions: How do I feel right now? Is this how I really want to feel, or do I want to feel_____? What would I have to believe in order to feel that way? What am I willing to do to make it happen? What can I learn from this?

4. Be confident: Recall a specific time when you felt a specific emotion or feeling and somehow got over it. How did you do it? Did something in your mindset shift? Remembering a time when you were able to deal with the emotion will reassure you that you can deal with it now.

5. Be certain: Imagine coming up with diverse ways of handling this emotion. If one does not work, try another. Keep trying until you feel confident.

6. Now let's get excited and take action: Do something right away that shows you can handle your emotions. Express your emotion in a way that reinforces what you have rehearsed in your mind and changes the way you feel.

You can't merely "consume" personal development or success. You actually have to DO it. It's time to start connecting with your own journey.

If you ever read the book "The Secret" or anything about the Law of Attraction, you know that when we ask for something, believe it is coming, and are open to receive it, it will manifest. The same applies when you work on mastering your emotions.

We are all on this journey to a bigger life, and along the way it is inevitable that we will experience that feeling of stress. What will set you apart is how you develop your ability to manage stress. These tools will guide you and help you in that direction to a more peaceful and meaningful life.

IV. Positive Self-Talk vs. Negative Self-Talk

One way to direct your focus is through positive self-talk. Negative self-talk not only increases stress; it also creates resistance, which will prevent you from achieving a goal at which you could otherwise succeed. Positive self-talk helps you calm down and control stress. Self-talk can be as simple as listening to what you are saying to yourself each day and bringing awareness to those thoughts. With practice, you can learn to turn negative thoughts into positive ones. For example, inner dialogue changes from "I'll never get well" or "I'm so stupid" to "I can do this," or "Things will work out." Statements like "Everything is going wrong" can become "I can handle things if I take it one step at a time."

Instead of saying, "I hate it when this happens," remind yourself that, "I know how to deal with this; I've done it before." Use positive self-talk to remind yourself that there is no such thing as perfect, for example, "I can't do that," becomes "I will try the best I can."

V. Writing Tools

Keeping a Journal and Stress Diary:

As mentioned in Chapter 1, journaling allows you to purge and process negative emotions and events. In doing so you will begin to recognize the lens through which you view life events; this new awareness will in turn help you shift your perspective. Similarly, keeping a stress diary for a few weeks is an effective stress management tool as it will help you become more aware of the situations which cause you to become stressed. Note down the date, time and place of each stressful episode, and note what you were doing, who you were with, and how you felt both physically and emotionally. Use the diary to understand what triggers your stress and how effective you are in stressful situations. This will enable you to avoid stressful situations and develop better coping mechanisms.

Problem-solving Technique:

This is a close cousin to journaling and keeping a stress diary. When using the problem-solving technique, you write down your challenge, dilemma, et cetera and come up with as many possible solutions as you can. Decide on the good and bad points of each one and select the best solution. Write down each step that you need to take as part of the solution: what will be done, how will it be done, when will it be done, who is involved, and where will it take place. Also remember that you are in control of your own actions, decisions, and choices. Do not enter any situation or make any decisions that will later leave you feeling stressed about it.

VI. Positive Intent

You can also think of a stressor in your life you'd like to change or simply understand. I'd like you to think about that stress, and just for a moment, touch the part of your body where you think that stress resides. What ignites that stress, that emotion, inside you? Trust your intuition, your first gut reaction. Where does it go? Where does it come from? As you are touching that body part, I want you to go inside and understand that everything has a reason. Even though it may not look very pretty right now, this stress has a reason or what's called a positive intent, and you can learn to appreciate it. Remember, the more you resist something, the more it continues. The more you fight, the more it fights back, so you just get caught up in that fight and nothing changes. Doing this exercise helps us learn to appreciate stress for what it can teach us, and manage it in a positive way so it doesn't get the better of us. When you understand the reason or positive intent behind the stress you are faced with, you're trusting that it's there to serve you, even though it hurts at the moment.

VII. Meditation

Sit quietly, in a place you will not be disturbed. Be sure to turn off your phone, computer, television, et cetera. Begin by focusing on your breath, deeply inhaling and exhaling. If a person or event in the day has upset you, reflect constructively on those situations. Examine what emotions are coming up, close your eyes, and notice what sensations you have in your body.

Focus your attention on the part of your body that feels the feeling; describe the feeling. For example, is it a pit in your stomach? Tightness in your chest? Grinding of your teeth? Is it an overall feeling, like fatigue? Are you upset? Angry? Frustrated? Disappointed? What part of your body is feeling these emotions? Send love and to that part of the body and thank it for helping to make you aware of your feelings.

Now, return to your thoughts. When we are feeling stressed, we tend to overthink the situation, and they usually involve limiting beliefs. Meditation is a great way to replace the negative thoughts.

VIII. 10-Day Challenge

This is how you create a level of choice instead of a reaction that is an everyday pattern for you. First identify the emotions, feelings, and stress that you experience most often. Then, find a new word or words that help you to break your pattern of thought and feeling. Avoid "I am" statements because these are powerful identifiers and will further bind you to the emotion. Instead use words like "I am noticing that…" This tool gives you the power to change your experiences about stress; it also helps create beneficial habits that will change your life for the better.

IX. Tools for Dealing with Parenting Stress

Give your kids things they can own and control.

- Engage your children in their own upbringing. Research backs this up—children who plan their own goals, set weekly schedules,

and evaluate their own work take more control over their lives. We have to let our children succeed on their own terms, and yes, on
occasion, fail on their own terms. We must
remember we are dealing with kids, not ma-
ture adults; they are still learning, and it is
up to us to stay calm and collected during
stressful situations. Otherwise we will raise
kids who stress easily into adulthood.

Don't worry about raising happy kids.

- Focus on raising productive kids with morals
  and integrity. Hope that happiness will come
  to them by virtue of the good they do and the
  love that they feel from us.

Value who they are as people.

- We teach our kids how to love. They cannot
  love others if they do not first love themselves
  and they won't love themselves if we can't
  offer them unconditional love. When our kids
  come home from school or we come home
  from work, we need to unplug from technol-
  ogy, put away our phones, look them in the
  eye, and let them see the joy that fills our fac-
  es when we see them. Ask them, "How was
  your day? What did you like about today?"

Let them know how much they matter to you.

Teach your kids to help around the house—without being asked

- Our kids learn their work ethic from us. Many parents either excuse their kids from doing chores around the house or give them a list of chores. This leads them to have no accountability or unable to take initiative because they are always waiting for someone to hand them a checklist. They lack the impulse or instinct to roll up their sleeves, look around and ask themselves, "How can I be useful to co-workers? How can I anticipate a few steps ahead to what my boss might need?" Teach them early on to do things without being asked, for example offering help to someone struggling with grocery bags or trying to open a door.

X. Stress Through Communication

As a life coach I have worked with people who cannot speak up for themselves or assert their boundaries. This was the case with Amy; her boundaries were non-existent, which translated into allowing the people in her life to do anything they wished to her.

People who face this problem are being disrespected, devalued, and trampled on, in work and in their personal lives. They find that they simply can't tell their boss, "No, this doesn't work" or "No, this behavior has to stop because it's toxic and damaging"; in their personal lives they find it difficult to speak up to their spouse or family member and say, "I don't appreciate being treated that way." This inability affects our emotional, physical, and behavioral functioning.

As is often the case, this problem stemmed from Amy's childhood, but she carried the effects of it well into adult life. Our beliefs and behavior around communication come from how we were trained and treated in our childhood. Everything you experienced as you attempted to develop and assert your boundaries as a child and teen has affected you deeply, unless you've done the work to revise it, heal it, and change it. Over the years I have noticed that speaking up powerfully for oneself is one of the most universal challenges human beings face today.

It is never too late to learn to speak up for yourself and advocate for your own needs, values, and wishes. Your feelings are valid and should be acknowledged and respected, especially by co-workers, friends, and family. As with the other tools in this book, take it step by step and celebrate each success. Before you know it you will notice a dramatic shift in your life.

XI. Last but not least, here are four techniques that research has shown help to reduce stress in the short- and long-term, as well as the health consequences it causes

Take a break from the stressor. It may seem difficult to get away from your crying baby, growing bills, a big project at home or at work. But when you give yourself permission to step away from it, you are allowing your brain to decompress, which can help you shift your perspective. It also frees up time for healthy practices that reduce feelings of overwhelm. This is not about avoiding the source of your stress (those bills have to be paid sometime; the project has to get finished; and the baby needs attention) but even just twenty minutes of self-care can work wonders.

Exercise. We keep hearing about the long-term benefits of a regular exercise routine. This is certainly true, however, even a twenty-minute walk, run, swim or dance session in the midst of a stressful time can give an immediate effect that can last for several hours.

Smile and laugh. Our brains are interconnected with our emotions and facial expressions. When people are stressed, they often hold a lot of the stress in their face. Some people wear their heart on their sleeve, which means they cannot hide their emotions. Laughing and smiling helps relieve some of that tension and improve the situation. Go to a comedy show or watch a funny movie. You will be surprised by how therapeutic this is. If you need an extra incentive, it is also proven that laughing burns calories!

Get social support. Call a friend, send an email. Sharing your concerns or feelings with another person is a proven stress-reliever. Just be sure that the person you talk to is someone you trust and can understand and validate you. If your family is a stressor, for example, it may not alleviate your stress if you share your stress with one of them. Find positive people who will motivate you.

Acknowledgements

I would like to acknowledge "My circle"—you know who you are. Your faith in me has pushed me to try harder and continue to have faith in myself.

I want to thank my friends and family, who in their own way each helped make this book possible.

I acknowledge my clients who helped me see the various ways stress can manifest in someone's life and for giving me the opportunity to provide them with tools to build their own solid foundation. You all have come a long way and will continue to do so.

To Sue Urda of Powerful You! Publishing and my editor Dana Micheli, for believing in my dream, helping me accomplish this goal, and being there for me throughout the process.

Lin Moctezuma

Connect with Lin

Website linlifecoach.com

Email: linlifecoach@gmail.com

Facebook: facebook.com/linthelifecoach

Instagram: LinTheLifeCoach

Twitter: @linthelifecoach

About the Author

The world is not all sunshine and rainbows, but with the right tools you can manage the gray areas and the rainy days.

Lin Moctezuma is a Certified Life Coach who specializes in Stress Management and building powerful relationships. In addition to her one-on-one coaching sessions, Lin hosts stress management workshops to teach people the tools they need to handle stress in a more positive way.

Lin graduated from the Robbins-Madanes Training/RMT Center Core 100 program, where she obtained her Life Coaching Certification. She has also trained at the Center for Coaching Certification, as well as other coaching programs.

Lin's personal journey has included many challenges and victories; it also led her to discover her passion for helping others overcome their own obstacles. She is known by her clients not only for her effective tools, but for her outgoing, kind-hearted, ambitious, nurturing, and compassionate coaching style. In her spare time, Lin enjoys reading, writing, and entertaining in her home.

Are You Called to be an Author?

If you're like most people, you may find the prospect of writing a book daunting. Where to begin? How to proceed? No worries! We're here to help.

Whether you choose to contribute to an anthology or write your own book, we'll be your guiding light, professional consultant, and enthusiastic supporter. If you can see yourself as an author partnering with a publishing company who has your best interest at heart and with the expertise to back it up, we'd be honored to be your publisher.

We provide personalized guidance through the writing and editing process. We offer complete publishing packages and our service is designed for a personal and optimal authoring experience.

We are committed to helping individuals express their voice and shine their light into the world. Are you ready to start your journey as an author? Do it with Powerful You! Publishing.

Powerful You! Publishing
239-280-0111
powerfulyoupublishing.com

MANAGE YOUR STRESS MASTER YOUR LIFE

CPSIA information can be obtained
at www.ICGtesting.com
Printed in the USA
LVHW022248060820
662367LV00017B/555